How to use this book:

We sincerely appreciate your purchase of our meticulously crafted ephemera book. This collection, artfully generated with Ai to serve as a versatile resource for a wide range of creative endeavors, and we'd like to offer some professional and innovative suggestions on how to maximize its potential:

-Papercraft Artistry: Explore the depths of your creativity by using these images to create intricate and captivating papercraft artworks.

-Junk Journaling: For those who love the art of storytelling through visuals, these images are perfect for embellishing your junk journals.

-Scrapbooking Mastery: Elevate your scrapbooking game by incorporating our ephemera.

-Decoupage Brilliance: Achieve a seamless blend of vintage by using these images in your decoupage projects.

-Creative Card Making: Craft unique and memorable cards for any occasion with the help of our ephemera.

-Mixed Media Magic: Combine various mediums and techniques to create mixed media artworks that tell beautiful stories.

To ensure you make the most of this collection, consider the following tips:

Precise Cutting: When removing images from the book, use sharp, precise cutting tools to maintain the integrity of the designs.

We hope you derive immense joy and satisfaction from working with our ephemera. May your creative journey be as enchanting as the images themselves.

Happy crafting!

100% NATURAL
CUCUMBER

ORGANIC BEST
ONION

TOMATO
FARM FRESH

ECO FOOD
EGGPLANT FRESH

CARROT
BEST

POTATO
100% ORGANIC

Best For
YOUR
DINNER

Keep Healthy
JUST
DRINK
Strawberry

Always there
FOR YOU

EAT ALL
you can
START FROM $5

Triple Combo
BURGER
ONLY $30

Good Food for
HAPPINESS

COFFEE
for everyone
BUY 2 GET 1

Choose Your
BREAKFAST
OR
PANCAKE   WAFFLE

Uncle Ben's
PASTRAMI
20%

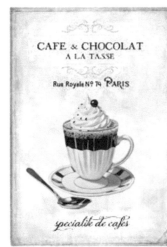

CAFE & CHOCOLAT
A LA TASSE

Rue Royale N° 74 PARIS

spécialité de cafés

CAFE
de Paris

Goutez & comparez ! Qualité sans Rivale.

45, Rue de Cléry, PARIS

Prenez à votre déjeuner
+
PATISSERIE
+

SPÉCIALITÉ
MACARONS

SPÉCIALITÉ
DE
Patisserie

MAISON A PARIS
28, Rue St Sulpice

1960

TEAS
& COFFEES

1960

TEA

The Victoria Tea Company

SPÉCIALITÉ
DE
Patisserie

MAISON A PARIS
28, Rue St Sulpice

SPÉCIALITÉ
MACARONS
+
PATISSERIE

MARQUE DE FABRIQUE

Maison a Paris, art 290

Cherry cupcake

VANILLA
CUPCAKES

Chocolat, Cacao, Dragées, Confiserie

SPÉCIALITÉ
DE TRUFFES

Entrepôts généraux :
PARIS, 41, rue des Francs-Bourgeois.
LONDRES, 39, Holborn Viaduct, E.C.
NEW-YORK, 13, Warrenstreet.

Lemon Cream
CUPCAKE
RECIPE

Chocolate
CUPCAKES

crème
Patisserie

PARIS, BOULEVARD SEBASTOPOL, 18

Cherry cupcake
RECIPE

VANILLA
CUPCAKES

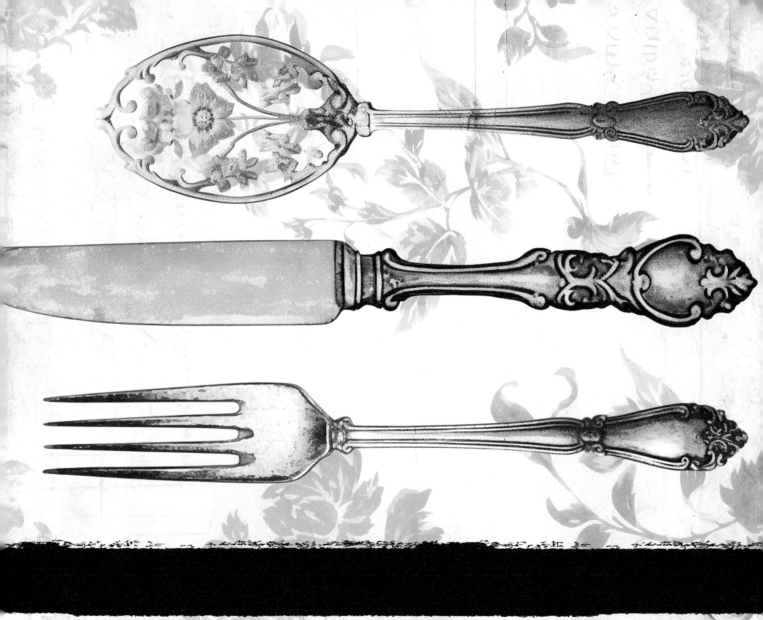

JAPANESE CUISINE

Sushi

Nigiri Sushi is one of the most popular types of sushi. It is fish served on rice seasoned lightly with vinegar

Okonomiyaki

A dish in which vegetables, meat, seafood and other ingredients are added to a mixture of wheat flour, egg, water and cooked on a hotplate

Takoyaki

It is a Japanese snack in the shape of little round balls. It is typically filled with minced or diced octopus, tempura scraps, red pickled ginger, and green onion

Tonkatsu

It is a dish based on western pork cutlets, where a thick slice of pork coated with flour and dipped in beaten egg, coated in breadcrumbs and fried in oil

Miso-shiru

It is the standard Japanese soup seasoned with miso and made with tofu, wakame and daikon

Tempura

The batter-coated seafood and vegetables are traditionally fried in oil

Sashimi

It is thinly sliced fresh raw fish, such as salmon or tuna—that is served without rice

Unagi

It is eel grilled over charcoal and basted with sweet soy sauce

Ramen

It consists of Ramen or Chinese noodles served in a meat or fish-based broth, often flavored with soy sauce, miso or salt with different toppings

Made in United States
Troutdale, OR
07/25/2024

21528231R00029